Sweet Surprise or Sour Secret?

This book belongs to

....

ISBN 979-8-88869-608-8

Things Kids Must Know

APURVA
KAUSHIK SHARMA

INDIA • SINGAPORE • MALAYSIA

FOREWORD

As parents we want to protect our children from the world, however, as superhuman as we feel, we can't be everywhere. In a world of good and bad, safe and unsafe the only way to protect your child is to empower them to know right from wrong, and help them develop a moral compass.

This book is a tool to empower your child with the knowledge of body safety. The book is based on the author'slearnings from interaction with thousands of children and care givers from varied socio-economic backgrounds about the challenges they face in different settings. In my experience as a lawyer and human rights activist, the only way forward is to educate and empower the coming generations of their rights from their early years.

Besides teaching them about right from wrong, it is also important to inform them about the recourse available to them. In any situation, the first step is to identify the problem and the second step is to provide a solution for it. One would be surprised to know that the best defence we can offer our children is awareness, it is only when they are aware and know how to identify a problem that we can help them solve it.

I am sure this book will serve you as a steppingstone in your journey to empower your child.

– Ms Laavanya Kaushik (Lawyer)

Hi, I am Harry! Meet my friends Sara and Aditya.
We go to school together and we love to play.
Sara and Aditya like to paint, while I like to read.
So, when they are painting, I read.
We spend most of our time together.

Aditya is always happy and full of energy.
He is a caring friend and shares everything with me.
Out of the three of us, I would say Sara
is the naughty one, but she is also very kind.
I always tell them how I feel
and they always listen to me.
I love my friends!

Last week Aditya won the first prize in a painting competition at school.
He was very happy and excited.
He is quite talented
and we are all very proud of him.

Though, Aditya has stopped playing with us for the last two days.
He is always sad. He looks lost in school also.

Sara and I are worried about him.
I have tried many times to go to his house and talk to him, but he never talks to me.
I have decided that Sara and I will surely speak with him today.

Harry and Sara go to Aditya's house and take his mother's permission to talk to him. She has also been worried about him and is happy to know that Harry and Sara want to help.

Harry: Aditya! Please tell us why you are so sad. Why don't you play with us? Is something wrong? Don't worry! You can trust us and tell us anything.

Aditya suddenly started crying and hugged Harry. He said, "Last weekend, my uncle came to stay with us and he used to sleep in my room. While sleeping, he used to touch me between the legs."

"I was so confused and annoyed with him,
but I didn't know what to do.
I thought it was my mistake and was scared of
telling anyone about it.
He said it was our secret game and that
nobody would believe me even if I told anyone."

Harry: Oh God, Aditya! Why didn't you
tell me earlier? My mom warned me about this.
What uncle did to you was an unsafe touch!
You must tell aunty.

She will talk to your uncle and report him.
He is not allowed to do that. It is wrong!
Sara: Yes! It is not your fault Aditya.
Don't be scared.
Please, you should tell aunty.
Harry and Sara explain to
Aditya's mother what happened.
She goes to Aditya, wipes his tears and hugs him.

Aditya's mother: You don't have to be scared, Aditya.Why didn't you tell me before?
Aditya: Ma! Uncle said it was our secret bedtime game.
I should not tell anyone about it.
Aditya's mother: There is no such secret!
You don't have to keep secrets from dad or me.
You must tell me if something happens that scares or confuses you.

Aditya: But Mumma, we had kept dad's surprise birthday party a secret!?

Aditya's mother: Surprises are different from secrets.

Surprises are fun things, they make us feel happy and will always be told.

Like if you have a surprise birthday party it makes everyone happy and you don't tell anyone about it only until the party.

On the other hand, secrets can make us feel sad, scared or confused.

If someone asks us to keep a secret, they will ask us never to tell the secret to anyone. Like uncle did, but you must not keep a secret like this.

Aditya's mother: I will teach uncle a lesson and report him.
How dare he! Give me the phone!
I am going to call 1098.
Aditya's mother calls 1098 (Childline) to report his uncle and his wrongdoing.

Harry and Sara hug Aditya.

Hi! I will tell you about
Safe & Unsafe touch
and how to keep yourself safe.

Safe touch is a touch
that makes us feel happy,
warm and loved.
It is allowed!

Such as:
When our parents hug us.
When our friends hug us.
When our teacher pats us on the back,
when we do a good job.

We are kids, but we are the boss of our body!
We have body parts like eyes, ears,
legs, hands, etc., which are visible to others
even after we wear clothes.

We also have private parts. Private means one's own and the parts covered by a swimming costume or our undergarments are our private parts.

No one is allowed to touch them, look at them or talk about them.

Our mouth is visible to everyone, but it is also our private part, so no one is allowed to touch it.

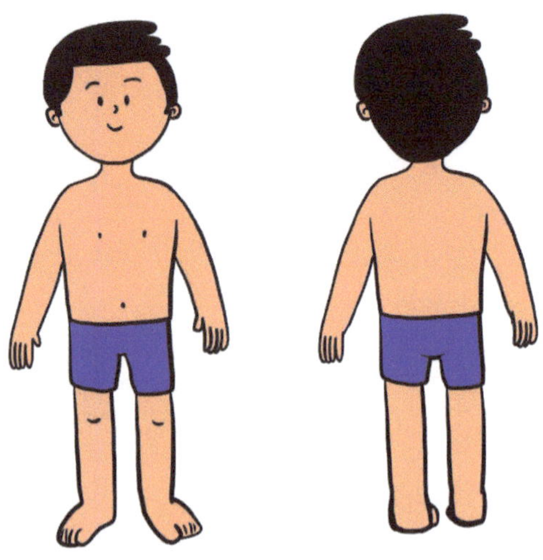

Body parts covered by a swimming costume or undergarments are our private parts, as shown .
Our mouth is also our private part.

As we are the boss of our body,
we can also decide who comes close to us.
We have a boundary around our
body that we can't see, which no one
can enter without our permission.
It's called a body bubble,
as shown in the picture below.

People are not allowed to enter your
body bubble if you don't want them to.

What should you do if you
don't feel like hugging??
We can say," No, How about a high five?"
and give them a high five.

We can also shake hands with them.

If someone touches our private parts,
it is an Unsafe touch.
It makes us feel scared,
confused or bad.
It is not allowed.
We shout "NO" and get away from that person.
When a person asks you to keep the
"touch" a "secret", it is unsafe.
When a person hides that they touched you.
It is unsafe.
It is not your fault.

When to say NO!

If someone talks about private parts
We shout "NO"

If someone touches our prvate parts
We shout "NO"
If someone asks us to touch their
private parts
We shout "NO"

If someone looks at our private parts
We shout "NO"
If someone asks us to look
at their private parts
We shout "NO"

If someone shares pictures of
themselves without clothes
We shout "NO"
If someone asks for your picture.
We say "NO"

It is okay to say "NO" to people we know too
if they make us feel unsafe.

Safe touch
Makes us feel :
Happy
Cared for
Loved
Warm
Comfortable

Unsafe touch
Makes us feel :
Scared
Confused
Yucky
Sad
Uncomfortable

ALWAYS REMEMBER!

- YOU should not keep unsafe touch a secret.
- If someone touches your private parts, you say NO and GET AWAY/RUN.
- You go to a member of your Safety Circle and tell them about it to get HELP. (Choose your safety circle on the next page!)
- You keep asking for help until you get it.
- You can call 1098, a 24 hours helpline for children called Childline. You can call them at any time, day or night.

1098

- You can also dial 100, the Police, they are also there for you always.

The safety circle is the circle of adults you trust and feel safe with. They are your Grown-up Buddies, and they will not make you feel unsafe. They always protect you and always be there to help you.

Parenting tip:
Make your child identify 4 to 5 grown-up buddies who will be a part of their Safety circle. It is preferred to have 1 person in the circle from outside the family.

Safety tip: Never keep an unsafe touch/situation a secret.

Safety tip: Keep asking for help until you get it. Be strong and don't be scared.

Safety tip: Stranger is danger but a known person can also make you feel unsafe. You should ask for help then too.

Safety tip: Always change your clothes in private. If your parents help you wear/change your clothes, ask them to do it where nobody can see you.

Safety tip: If anyone shows you pictures of people without clothes, ask them not to.
Tell a member of your Safety Circle!

Safety tip: Safety tip: You should always visit the doctor with your parents/a safety circle member. The doctor is allowed to check your private parts if required, but in the presence of your parents/a safety circle member only.

Safety tip: It is okay if your parents help you bathe and clean your body parts.

LET'S PLAY THE SAFETY BINGO

Tick if you know

I know my private parts	I know what is a safe touch (give your mum a hug)	I know what is an unsafe touch
I know I have to say NO to an unsafe touch and GET AWAY	I know which is my Safety Circle, for help	I will never keep an unsafe touch a secret even if I am asked to
I am strong and intelligent.	I know I am the boss of my body.	I can take care of myself

BINGO!!!

You now know how to stay safe

Now, use the sample postcard on the next page to inform your chosen Grown-up buddies that they are part of your Safety Circle.

Dear ....

Hope you are doing well. Recently I
learnt how to stay safe and take care of myself.
I also learnt that I should have a Safety
Circle of my most trusted and helpful adults,
my Grown-up Buddies. And guess what?
I have chosen you as my Grown-up buddy!

Now you must help me whenever
I ask for it and promise that you'll listen
to me and believe me.

I hope you will become a part of my Safety Circle.

Thank you
Lots of love

....

ADD YOUR PICTURE HERE

PLACE STAMP HERE

Parents' guide

Hi, this book is a step towards making the conversation on body safety easier and more comfortable for both children and parents. As parents, we can't be present at all times to ensure our children's safety and supervise them. The aim is to enable you to introduce your child to body safety in his/her early years.

Why is it essential to talk about it?

- Children typically experience abuse at the hands of the people they know.
- They lack the vocabulary to explain such experiences and are often confused about what happened. Thus, they don't ask for help and the abuse continues.
- They should be able to identify unsafe encounters for themselves.
- Child abuse has long-lasting implications on the child's development and behaviour.
- Only when we remove the inhibitions and taboo attached, can we create safe spaces for the child to talk about it and give them the much-needed constructive help.

When is the right time to explain the "privacy" of private parts?

When the child starts going to school or you start leaving them in the care of others. It is a must for them to know the difference between safe and unsafe situations and touch.

They need:

1. To learn to first identify the safe from the unsafe.
2. To have a safety strategy for themselves.

In the long run, it will help them as they venture into the world. They will learn to deal with various kinds of people and navigate through uncomfortable situations.

How to use the book?

Read this book to your child and discuss it in detail, giving examples and situations of your daily life and surroundings. Parents know what is best for their children and are their guide and confidant. Here are a few reading tips that will make your child understand their body safety better.

Reading tips:

- Do not feel awkward; introduce it as a safety guideline to your child. Remember, talking about an unsafe touch is as basic and essential as telling your child not to touch a hot pan/a knife.
- Read the book during the day.
- There are a few fun activities at the end of the book. Help your child complete the activities. It will make him/her understand it better.
- Read it to your child again after 2 months.

Keep a two-way communication while reading. Ask your child what they are thinking. Discuss various situations like people they interact with while going to school, things they do when you are away and another person babysits them. Remember, every child has an environment unique to them, and their interactions also vary from family to family. So, only a parent can best discuss various scenarios and "what-ifs" that require attention.

Happy reading!

www.ingramcontent.com/pod-product-compliance
Lightning Source LLC
LaVergne TN
LVHW021352160826
845679LV00008B/1586

* 9 7 9 8 8 8 8 6 9 6 0 8 8 *